HOW TO BE AN ECO EXPLORER

HOW TO BE AN ECO EXPLORER
Yussef Rafik
Illustrated by Holly Astle

First published in the UK and USA in 2025
by Moon + Bird, an imprint of Watkins Media Limited
Unit 11, Shepperton House, 83–89 Shepperton Road
London N1 3DF

info@moonandbirdbooks.com

Commissioning Editor: Lucy Carroll
Project Editor: Brittany Willis
Copyeditor: Claire Baker
Head of Design: Karen Smith
Illustrator: Holly Astle
Production: Uzma Taj

A CIP record for this book is available from the British Library

ISBN: 978-1-78678-869-6 (Hardback)
ISBN: 978-1-78678-920-4 (eBook)

10 9 8 7 6 5 4 3 2 1

Printed in China

www.moonandbirdbooks.com

MIX
Paper | Supporting responsible forestry
FSC® C136333

HOW TO BE AN ECO EXPLORER

YUSSEF RAFIK

BBC presenter of *Earth Kids*

Illustrated by Holly Astle

MOON BIRD

TOP TIP

Some of the activities in this book use plastic such as elastics and plastic bottles. To be an extra special eco explorer, you could look for more eco-friendly versions of these, such as biodegrabale tape. If you can't find any alternatives that are better for the environment, try reusing things you already own!

CONTENTS

INTRODUCTION

Planet Earth is a wonderful place to live. It's full of all different kinds of environments that support lots of amazing wildlife, all interacting with each other and depending on one another for survival.

We currently know of about 1.7 million different species of **organism** living on Earth, but scientists are discovering new living things all the time. The actual number of different species alive right now could be in the tens of millions. The fact that we have such rich variety, known in science as **biodiversity**, on our planet makes us incredibly lucky.

Sadly though, many of our plants, animals, and other wildlife are being put at risk by humankind. While most of us would not wish to harm nature, lots of things we do every day may be having an impact on the planet without us even realizing. The way that we consume products and live our lives can contribute to wildlife threats such as deforestation, climate change, pollution, and **habitat** loss.

It's now more important than ever to be aware of these problems and help to fight against them. However, massive global issues like these can feel rather scary and can often leave us with feelings of worry and helplessness. This is something called eco anxiety, and if you feel this way you are most definitely not alone.

Rather than focusing on these huge issues, it can be more helpful to think about smaller ways you and your family could help the environment around you.

And that's where this book comes in—it's full of activities we can do to make a positive change. It doesn't matter how small, these changes will have a positive impact on the planet. By learning about our natural world and doing as many of the activities as you can, you'll be a top-notch **eco explorer** in no time!

Being an eco explorer isn't about having expensive equipment and special clothes. We can be just as great an eco explorer dressed in sneakers and a sweatshirt as we can in a fancy coat and rain boots. Being an eco explorer is more about our mindset; it's about being aware of our behaviors, trying to promote **sustainability**, and educating others by raising awareness.

From rainforests to deserts and grasslands to oceans, this book looks at some of the many magnificent **ecosystems** that make up planet Earth, each one supporting a whole host of special wildlife with its own **food chain**, and each one facing threats of its own.

Humans live all over the world, so some of us will come across certain ecosystems more than others. It doesn't matter where you live though, because the actions we take in our local area can affect other habitats all over the world. Let's find out what we can do to help!

Here are some key terms you need to know before you get started on your eco explorer adventures. You'll find more terms in the glossary on pages 90–93.

ECO EXPLORER
Someone who gets stuck into nature and helps protect the planet.

HABITAT
The area where an organism lives.

ORGANISM
The name we give to any form of life. It could be a plant, an animal, a fungus, or even bacteria.

BIODIVERSITY
The variety of different organisms living in a particular habitat.

FOOD CHAIN
The order that organisms eat each other in an ecosystem, showing how living things depend on each other for food.

ECOSYSTEM
A community of lots of different organisms that live and interact with each other in a certain area.

SUSTAINABILITY
Using resources in a way that keeps them around for the future and doesn't harm the planet.

YARDS

Yards are important wildlife habitats because we can have the biggest impact in them. By using just a few simple eco explorer tricks we can turn them into gorgeous ecosystems filled with all kinds of fantastic creatures.

DID YOU KNOW?

In towns and cities, yards are even more important because they are often some of the most biodiverse places found there.

ADVENTURE CHALLENGE

With an adult, see how many different creepy-crawlies you can find in your yard or local park.

DID YOU KNOW?

Yards provide a fantastic place to rest for birds who fly long distances to other parts of the world for different seasons (known as migrating).

DID YOU KNOW?

Being outside in nature helps to calm our minds and is great for our mental wellbeing.

Yards come in so many different shapes and sizes. You might have a massive one or a tiny one, or maybe you have a shared one or no yard at all but a small window box instead.

The truth is, it really doesn't matter what kind of yard you have. Big or small, all yards are valuable to wildlife and there are still plenty of things you can do with them.

Yards are an important habitat for wildlife and if you plan yours well, it can provide food, water, and shelter for the animals that live there. The more species in your yard, the more biodiverse it will be.

Look Out For:

Can you spot these creatures in your yard?

BIRDS
You might see lots of different kinds of birds in your yard, especially if you put out bird feeders. Look out for sparrows, finches, and starlings carrying materials to build a nest, like sticks and fluff.

INSECTS
There could be thousands of insect and creepy-crawly species in your yard, but you might need to get close to the ground to find some of them. Look under rocks, behind leaves, and in narrow cracks.

NOCTURNAL ANIMALS
These are animals that only come out at night, such as bats, owls, hedgehogs, and foxes. Go out after dark with an adult to see them, but be super quiet!

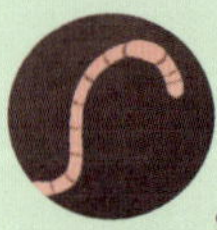

EARTHWORMS
Dig around in any soil and you'll find earthworms. They're a great food source for other animals, but they also do important work fertilizing the soil (see pages 56–63).

We've learned that yards are an important wildlife habitat, but they're also a great place for us to hang out, too. In an ideal world, all living creatures would enjoy yards together, but unfortunately, sharing this space often brings conflict instead.

★ ARTIFICIAL LAWNS (otherwise known as fake grass) might look good, but they harm habitats. They form a barrier that prevents underground wildlife (like earthworms) from reaching the surface, and above ground animals (like birds) from reaching the soil.

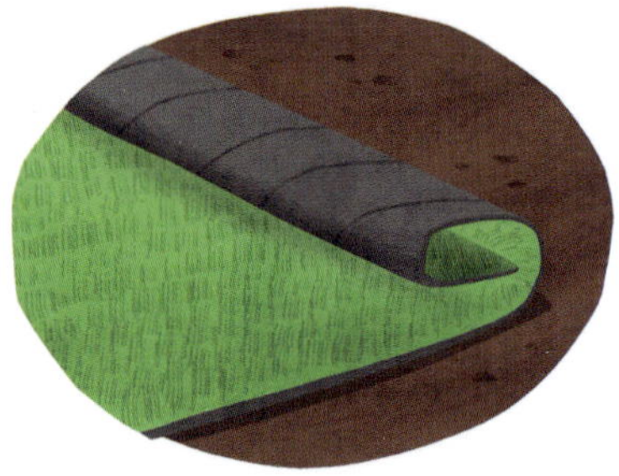

★ CHEMICAL PESTICIDES are substances that are often used to get rid of species that we consider pests (any organism that is harmful or annoying to humans or crops). The problem is that those pests are part of a food chain and by poisoning them, we also poison the animals that eat them.

★ INVASIVE SPECIES are organisms that come from elsewhere and are not local or native. Invasive species of plants may look pretty, but they compete with native plants that local wildlife relies on. Some, like Himalayan balsam, are so fast-growing that they stop native species from growing, too.

HABITAT HERO: WASPS

Wasps are known for being a bit of a nuisance, especially when you're trying to enjoy a cool ice lolly, but they are actually the unsung heroes of our yards. They hunt and eat many species of pests that munch on your valuable yard plants, such as flies, aphids, and caterpillars. A single wasp nest can consume many thousands of little pests every summer!

Our biggest mission as eco explorers is to coexist peacefully with wildlife, sharing our space and enjoying the company of nature. It's not always easy, but here are a few ways to attract wildlife to your yard:

ACTIVITY: BUILD A BUG HOTEL

Bugs are the hardest-working animals on the planet. Some bugs, called detritivores, break down waste. Others, called pollinators, help plants make new offspring by moving pollen between flowers. One in three mouthfuls of the food we eat was made because of pollinators.

Sadly, 41% of insects around the world are faced with extinction. Habitat loss is a big threat, so what better way to honor our minibeast friends than to build them bug hotel to live in.

A bug hotel is a safe space for bugs, where they can shelter from the weather and hide from predators. You can buy fancy bug hotels in most garden centers, but bugs aren't fussy about looks! The easiest way to build your own bug hotel is to use as many items that you can find outdoors or around your house as you can.

Eco Explorer Kit List:

- **Gardening gloves**
- **Secateurs**
- **Twigs**
- **Stones**
- **Bamboo cane**
- **Plant pot**
- **Loose bark**
- **Pine cones**
- **Fallen leaves**
- **String (optional)**

Step 1: Before you get started, remember to put on your gardening gloves. Ask an adult to help you chop your twigs and bamboo cane to the exact height of the plant pot.

Step 2: Turn the plant pot onto its side and begin piling up your stones inside.

Step 3: Poke in the twigs, bamboo cane, loose bark, pine cones, and fallen leaves as messily as you like.

Make sure the pot is jam-packed so that nothing falls out, adding in extra leaves to fill any gaps.

SAFETY FIRST:
Don't handle the secateurs without an adult present–they're very sharp!

Step 4: All that's left now is to choose the right position for your bug hotel in your yard. You'll get different residents depending on where you place it.

To attract bees, make sure you place it in a sunny spot. You could even attach some string to the top of your hotel and hang it on a fence.

If you want to attract creatures like woodlice and beetles, then place it somewhere cool and damp closer to the ground.

Now all you have to do is wait patiently for your first guests to arrive.

ACTIVITY: BUILD A WILDLIFE POND

The more biodiversity there is in your yard the better. Another great way to attract more creatures to a specific place is to build a pond.

Ponds are a fantastic water source for birds to bathe in and small mammals to drink from, but they also offer a home to amphibians and aquatic insects.

A pond doesn't have to be big or deep to attract wildlife. With just an old leak-proof tub, bucket, or container you can create a perfect pond—a dishpan will work. Choose a quiet spot in your yard to build your pond, preferably surrounded by lots of plants for animals to hide in.

Eco Explorer Kit List:

- **Spade**
- **Empty container**
- **Pebbles**
- **Piece of wood or slate**
- **Watering can**
- **Rainwater**
- **Pond plants**

Step 1: Use your spade to dig a hole in the ground roughly the size of your container. Then sink it into the hole, filling any gaps around the edge with the soil you dug up. If you are unable to dig into the ground, you can use your container to create a raised pond.

Step 2: Pour a layer of pebbles into the bottom of the container to give aquatic animals something to hide between.

Step 3: Add the wood or slate inside the container to make a ramp. This allows any animals that fall into your pond to escape and not drown. If you created a raised pond, you can also add a ramp on the outside to help animals get in.

Step 4: Now for the fun bit! Use a watering can to fill up your pond with water. Collect rainwater for this if you can. If not, tap water will work perfectly fine.

Step 5: Add your pond plants, which you can buy from most garden centers—choose native ones if possible. Plants help to add oxygen to the water and give the little aquatic animals places to hide.

Now keep a close eye on your pond and watch out for the first visitors to come and take a dip.

COASTS

Oceans cover 71% of the Earth's surface, providing a home to between 50–80% of all life on the planet. While some of us may not come into contact with oceans often, there's no doubt that they are a hugely important habitat and need our protection.

DID YOU KNOW?

There are an estimated 7,500,000,000,000,000,000 grains of sand on all of our beaches —that's a lot of zeros! To read this huge number aloud, say: seven quintillion five hundred quadrillion.

DID YOU KNOW?

Every year, around 14 million tons of plastic finds its way into our oceans, causing harm to countless numbers of sea creatures.

Coastlines, where the sea meets the land, come in many different forms depending on where you are in the world. A coastline could be a swamp, a marshland, or a sandy, pebble, or volcanic beach, but they all support life.

Coastal regions are an important part of the marine landscape because it's here that land ecosystems and aquatic ecosystems meet, meaning they are often rich in unique biodiversity.

DID YOU KNOW

The deepest part of the planet is the Mariana Trench in the Pacific Ocean. It's nearly 12,000 yards deep.

TOP TIP

At the beach, look out for sea glass, pretty pieces of broken glass that have been smoothed by the ocean's waves and washed ashore.

DID YOU KNOW?

There are over 230,000 known species of plants and animals currently living in our oceans.

ADVENTURE CHALLENGE

Next time you go to the beach, why not count how many different types of plants and animals you can spot?

Look Out For:

Can you spot these aquatic animals at the coast?

MARINE MAMMALS

If you look out to sea and are patient enough, you may see a marine mammal such as a dolphin, whale, or even a seal popping out of the water.

SEABIRDS

Coastlines can be home to birds you might not see anywhere else. Spot birds like gulls and cormorants in the sky, or wading birds like oystercatchers and plovers looking for tasty treats on the beach.

MERMAID'S PURSES

Search in the seaweed and you might come across a leathery pouch known as a mermaid's purse. It's actually an empty egg case that once held a baby shark or ray.

JELLYFISH

If you see a big, jelly-like blob on the beach it's actually a jellyfish! They can still sting you out of the water though, so don't touch them and just admire them from a distance.

Oceans and their coastlines make up one of the most important ecosystems on the planet, but they are also one of the most fragile. Humans rarely get close to marine life, but our lifestyle choices here on land have a big impact on it.

PLASTIC POLLUTION caused by millions of tons of single-use plastic finding its way into the ocean is a big problem. It takes hundreds of years to biodegrade (break down naturally), which means it's hard to get rid of it. It can even be found in the deepest parts of the Mariana Trench.

The plastic floating around in the ocean can get tangled and twisted around the poor sea creatures living there, and can even end up inside their stomachs. For example, a plastic bag may look like a tasty jellyfish to a sea turtle. Eating lots of plastic can sadly lead to the animal's death.

Even worse, the plastic can break down into smaller pieces called microplastics. These are eaten by animals at the bottom of the food chain and passed along to the predators that eat them.

HABITAT HERO: SEA SQUIRTS

Sea squirts are tube-shaped animals that live underwater and filter the water around them to feed on microscopic (tiny) plankton. Research has shown that sea squirts often remove harmful microplastics from the water at the same time, so they could even help to combat plastic pollution.

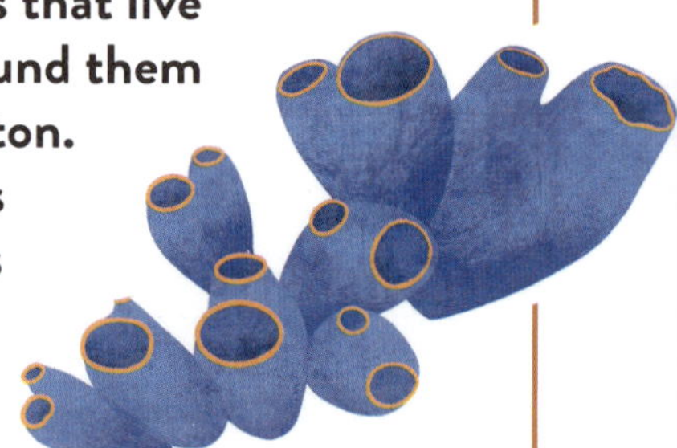

The massive issue of plastic pollution may seem daunting, but there are things you can do to reduce your single-use plastic consumption. Many chores around our homes are the responsibility of adults, so encouraging everyone you live with to help can make a big difference.

IN THE BATHROOM:

- Use bamboo toothbrushes that only take months to biodegrade. Plastic ones take years to disappear.
- Buy refillable shampoos to avoid buying new plastic bottles.
- Switch to soap bars—they don't use plastic in their packaging.
- Make your own cleaning products using vinegar and baking soda.

IN THE KITCHEN:

- Use reusable grocery bags.
- Bake homemade snacks instead of buying packaged ones.
- Drink out of a reusable water bottle to avoid throwing away lots of plastic bottles.
- Set up a compost bin (see pages 60–61) to reduce waste and fill fewer trash bags that go to the landfill.
- Use reusable containers or beeswax wraps instead of plastic.

WHEN DOING THE LAUNDRY:

- Encourage adults to use shorter washing machine cycles.
- Buy clothes made from cotton rather than synthetic fabrics like polyester.
- Sew and repair clothing instead of throwing it away.
- Donate any clothes that you no longer wear rather than putting them in the trash.

ACTIVITY: CARRY OUT A BEACH CLEAN

A great way to help the planet and prevent plastic from getting into the ocean is to carry out a beach clean.

To make it even more fun, why not encourage your friends to join you and compete to see who can find the most unusual item?

Keep your eyes peeled for rare treasures like teddy bears and Lego pieces. Once, thousands of rubber ducks spilled from a shipping container and washed up on beaches all around the world!

It's quite common for people doing beach cleans to find items such as toys or bags of chips from the 1980s. What's the oldest thing you can find on your beach clean?

Carrying out a beach clean is very simple—all you really need to do is grab your equipment, head to the nearest beach with an adult, and get to work.

Eco Explorer Kit List:

- **Gardening gloves**
- **Litter picker**
- **Collection bag/bucket**
- **Sturdy boots**

Here are a few things to keep in mind:

★ Don't pick up any sharp objects.

★ Plastic often gathers in the cracks and crevices of rocks, so this is a good place to look.

★ Be careful not to disturb the animals' habitat too much as you search for trash.

★ Once you've finished, be sure to dispose of the plastic responsibly and recycle what you can.

The more plastic you're able to remove from the beach the better, but don't worry about clearing the whole beach. Just collecting a handful of plastic and disposing of it properly in a trash can will have a positive impact.

ACTIVITY: MAKE A DIY BATHYSCOPE

A lot of the wildlife found at the coast lives below the surface of the water, which can make it tricky to spot. There is a really cool way to see them without getting wet or disturbing the animals. A bathyscope will allow you to see underwater creatures without getting your face wet.

Rock pools are the best place to find sea creatures at the beach, as a lot of animals shelter in them while they wait for the tide to come back in. They also make a great place to test out your DIY bathyscope. Here are a few rock pool creatures to look out for—how many can you find?

A bathyscope is the safest way to see underwater for both you and the creatures that live there. They are easy to make and allow you to reuse the plastic in your recycling box—which helps to make you the best eco explorer you can be.

Eco Explorer Kit List:

- **Wide plastic bottle (try to use an old one)**
- **Sharp scissors**
- **Clear plastic bag**
- **Rubber band or string**

Step 1: Ask an adult to cut the bottom off the wide plastic bottle with some scissors, then remove the bottle top.

Step 2: Stretch the clear plastic bag tightly over the bottom of the bottle, completely covering the opening you just made.

Step 3: Secure the bag with the rubber band. This end goes in the water, so make sure the band is really tight.

And now you have a bathyscope! Just lower the wider end with the plastic bag into the water, peer through the narrow end where the bottle top used to be and take an exciting peep at all the life below the water's surface.

SAFETY FIRST:

Never touch any sea creatures you find. Lots of them can sting or bite!

FORESTS

Forests cover almost 33% of all land on the planet and are extremely important habitats for lots of different organisms. They also play a big role in producing oxygen and fighting climate change.

DID YOU KNOW?

Every single minute, the world loses an estimated 35 acres of forest. That's over 17 soccer fields!

ADVENTURE CHALLENGE

Different forest tree species can be identified by their bark, leaves, and fruit. How many different species can you find locally?

During a process called photosynthesis, trees absorb carbon dioxide and remove it from the atmosphere. Too much carbon dioxide in the atmosphere makes the planet hotter, so forests are vital in limiting climate change.

There are many different types of forests worldwide:

TROPICAL RAINFORESTS
with warm and wet climates.

TEMPERATE FORESTS
with cooler temperatures and four seasons.

BOREAL FORESTS
which grow in frozen ground called permafrost.

All forests are havens for wildlife and are high in biodiversity. They offer a range of habitats, from the forest floor undergrowth to the high-up tree canopy.

They also provide safe places for animals to breed, nest, and hide from predators, and offer a variety of food sources, such as berries, insects, fruits, and nuts.

DID YOU KNOW?
Trees that lose their leaves in the fall, such as oaks, are called deciduous trees. Trees that keep their leaves all year round, such as pines, are called coniferous trees.

DID YOU KNOW?
Forests remove about 2.4 billion tons of carbon dioxide from the atmosphere every year.

DID YOU KNOW?
The oldest tree ever recorded is a bristlecone pine in California, USA. It's thought to be over 4,800 years old!

Ten thousand years ago, forests covered over half of all Earth's land. However, as the human population grew, so did our impact on the landscape. We have lost huge chunks of ancient forest to make room for things like agriculture, animal grazing, and housing.

★ DEFORESTATION is the process of cutting down large areas of forest. It's an increasing problem around the world, as trees are cut down to clear land and also to make wooden and paper products. Deforestation also leads to climate change because when trees are chopped down, all of the carbon dioxide they once absorbed is released back into the air. Around 10% of all global warming is caused by forest loss.

★ HABITAT LOSS is another major consequence of deforestation. If we chop down trees or plants, animals and fungi are at risk of dying off and becoming extinct.

HABITAT HERO: JAYS

Jays are a highly intelligent relative of the crow, known for hiding acorns in woodland. However, they often forget about their acorn stashes and so the acorns grow into oak trees, making jays great accidental tree-planters.

Look Out For:

Can you spot this nature in the forest?

BIRDS

Forests are full of diverse bird life because they provide everything birds may need: food, shelter, nesting materials, and safe places to build their nests.

MUSHROOMS

The nutrient-rich soils of forests make them a great place to find mushrooms of all different colors, shapes, and textures.

TREE SEEDS

The distinctive seeds of trees are often a lot bigger than other plant seeds. Acorns are oak tree seeds, conkers are from horse chestnut trees, and pine cones contain seeds from pine trees.

INVERTEBRATES

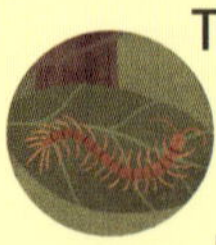

The dead wood on a forest floor makes the perfect dark, damp home for many invertebrates, which are animals without a bony skeleton. Lift up a piece of wood and look for centipedes, woodlice, slugs, and spiders hiding underneath.

It's difficult to fight deforestation when products made from trees are easily available. As consumers, it is easy to buy lots of products without thinking about where they came from and if the process of making them had a negative impact on the environment.

The first step to being an eco explorer is to be aware of the issues, then take measures to combat them. Here's some things to consider:

BUY SECOND HAND

Trees have to be cut down to make new wooden furniture, so it's much better to ask for second hand furniture for your room. Just paint or decorate it to make it look shiny and new!

AVOID PALM OIL PRODUCTS

Palm oil is found in many foods, cosmetics, and cleaning products, but cultivating it is a huge reason for deforestation, particularly in Southeast Asia and Africa. When shopping, check the ingredients on products and choose ones free from palm oil.

GO PAPERLESS

Paper is one of the main products made from trees. There are lots of recycled paper options out there but going completely paper-free is even better. For example, you can:

- Ask for birthday e-cards rather than paper ones.
- Read e-books instead of buying paper copies.
- Create digital art without using any paper.

EAT LESS MEAT

Making grazing space for the animals we eat is a huge cause of deforestation worldwide. Eating less meat helps to reduce the need for further deforestation.

TOP TIP

You don't need to give up meat altogether—even just having one meat-free day per week can help to make a difference.

ACTIVITY: GO BIRD WATCHING

Birds are an incredibly diverse group of animals that have evolved and adapted to live almost everywhere. This makes bird watching an activity that can be done anywhere, from yards to town centers. But to spot the most species, a forest is the place to be!

TRY NATURE BATHING
Lie on the forest floor, touch it with your hands, and take in the sights, sounds, smells, and textures of the natural world around you. This is calming and can help improve our mental wellbeing.

USE YOUR SENSES
Humans rely on sight as our primary sense, but in a forest it can be difficult to see birds. Luckily they are very vocal, so close your eyes and focus on the sounds of the forest instead.

Let's see how many species you can identify on your next bird-watching adventure. You can do this in your local forest or another outdoor space. On the right are some birds you may discover.

Eco Explorer Kit List:

- **Sturdy shoes**
- **Binoculars**
- **Bird identification book**
- **Pencil and notepad**

Step 1: Either sit down or walk around, remaining as quiet as possible so you don't disturb the birds.

Step 2: Listen for bird calls, then point your binoculars in that direction. Keeping an eye out for any movement can help you spot the bird.

Step 3: Use your book to try to identify the bird, jotting down all the different species you see in your notepad.

The more time you spend watching and listening to birds, the more you'll learn about their behaviors and become a fully-fledged bird expert.

TIME IT RIGHT

Start early! Birds are active all day but are noisiest during the early hours of the morning. The dawn chorus is like a beautiful orchestra as birds sing to attract mates and defend their territories.

Listen Out For:

Can you spot these birds by their unique sounds?

CUCKOOS
get their name from the distinct "cuck-coo" sound they make.

BARN OWLS
make a terrifying, long, loud screeching sound.

WOODPECKERS
create a drumming sound as they drill into trees with their beaks.

GREAT TITS
have a variety of calls, including a repetitive "tee-cher" sound.

CROWS
are intelligent birds with many different calls, including their distinctive "caw-caw".

PIGEONS
are well-known for their coo-ing sound.

TOP TIP

Identify the bird calls you hear more easily by making up phrases that they sound like. Perhaps a collared dove's coo sounds a bit like "hello-there"?

ACTIVITY: MAKE A FUNGUS SPORE PRINT

Fungi are organisms such as moulds, yeast, or mushrooms that reproduce using tiny particles called spores. They feed on decomposed natural materials and are important in lots of ecosystems because they provide food for many animals. Fungi also help break down rotting things, which is why we call them decomposers.

DID YOU KNOW?

Many mushrooms are poisonous so be careful when going near them! For example, the yellow mushroom below is called a fly agaric mushroom, and it's poisonous.

DID YOU KNOW?

Giant puffball mushrooms produce an average of seven trillion spores. That's more offspring than any other living thing on Earth produces!

Below the ground of the forest floor, a magical world exists known as the wood wide web. It's made up of intertwined fungal threads that create a complex network called a mycelium.

The trees can share food and water through the wood wide web. It's a fascinating example of plants and mushrooms communicating and working together.

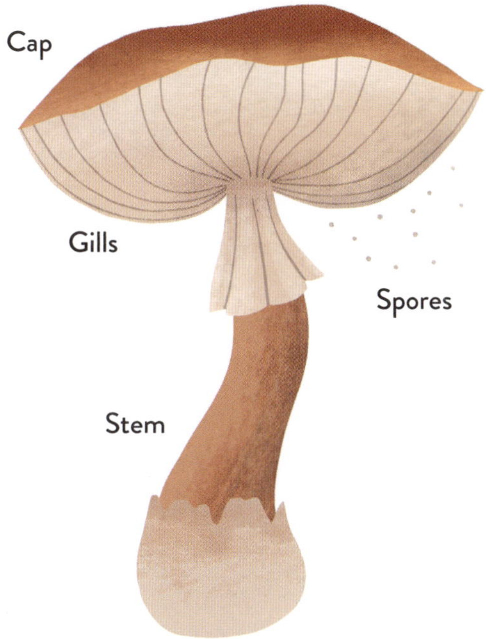

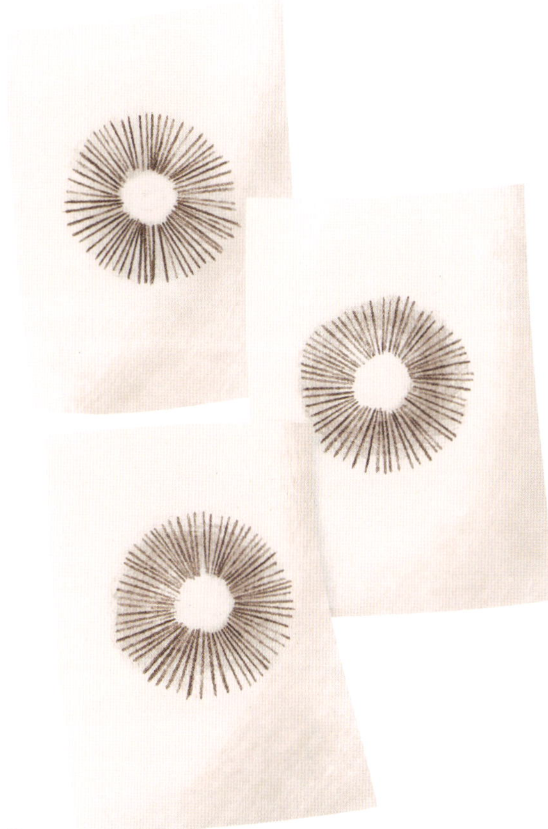

SAFETY FIRST:
Always wash your hands after touching wild mushrooms. Some mushrooms are poisonous so be careful not to put any near your mouth unless an adult has told you it's safe.

Fungi reproduce using spores, which are tiny particles in their gills. Spores blow away in the wind and get carried to new locations, where they grow into new mushrooms—but we can also use them to create works of art!

Eco Explorer Kit List:

- **Mushrooms**
- **Container**
- **Scissors**
- **Piece of paper**
- **Large bowl**

Step 1: Collect some wild forest mushrooms in your container and take them home. Make sure you do this with an adult as some mushrooms can be poisonous.

Step 2: Cut off the stems to leave just the mushroom caps, then place them onto the paper with the gills facing down. You could make a pattern by arranging different types of mushroom cap together.

Step 3: Cover all the laid-out mushrooms on the paper with a large bowl so that the caps don't dry out. Leave it like that overnight.

Step 4: Remove the bowl the next morning and lift off all the mushroom caps to reveal your spore print. Different species produce different colored spores, so it's exciting to see what you've created.

Now you've made your very own piece of fungal art. As well as being beautiful, spore prints can help us to identify the mushroom species it belongs to, a bit like fingerprints.

ARID CLIMATES

An environment is arid when it has very little rainfall, creating a dry landscape that's challenging for survival. A desert has less than 10 inches of rain a year, but many other places can be arid at times, for example during a very dry summer.

DID YOU KNOW?

The driest place on Earth is the Atacama Desert in Chile. Some parts haven't had a single drop of rain since records began!

DID YOU KNOW?

Deserts cover up to 30% of Earth's land surface and provide habitats for thousands of species of plants and animals.

DID YOU KNOW?

Some animals will dig a burrow to sleep in during the day because it's much cooler underground.

Many plants and animals have adapted so they can survive in a drought—we call them xerophiles. Here are some examples:

AFRICAN LUNGFISH
burrow into a drying riverbed and only re-emerge when it rains and the river refills (possibly months later). This is called estivation.

NOCTURNAL ANIMALS
come out at night when it's cooler, such as fennec foxes. That way they lose less water from their bodies through evaporation.

CAMELS
have humps that store fat, which is then broken down for energy when food and water is scarce.

OLIVE TREES
have a waxy coating on their leaves that helps to prevent water loss through evaporation.

SAGEBRUSHES
have tiny hairs on their leaves that trap moisture from the air.

CACTI
have fleshy stems to store water, and shallow roots to absorb rainwater as quickly as possible.

In arid times, some animals alter their behaviors, and knowing this can help you spot them. They might stay in the shade or underground during the day to keep cool, spend more time seeking water, or migrate to wetter regions.

DID YOU KNOW?
The kangaroo rat never drinks! Instead, it gets all the moisture it needs from the seeds it eats.

ADVENTURE CHALLENGE

Look under rocks and logs for bugs avoiding the heat. Put down wet sponges or fruit to give them a drink.

Look Out For:

Can you spot these on a hot day?

BIRDS
They can't survive for long without water. If you put out a bowl of water, local thirsty birds might gather in your yard for a drink and a splash.

REPTILES
Snakes and lizards are cold-blooded creatures, so they rely on the sun to give them heat. On a hot day, you can find them out in the open, basking on a sun-soaked rock.

SPIKES
Plants lose water through their leaves, so some arid plants have turned their leaves into thin spikes to help conserve their water. Spikes also have the added benefit of preventing animals from eating them!

Sadly climate change is making dry places a lot drier, with droughts happening more often and lasting a lot longer. Droughts lead to water shortages, but they have several further effects, too.

★ Plants protect the soil as their root systems hold it together. When plants die due to drought, the soil is no longer held together by the plant roots and is now at risk of erosion. This is when wind and water breaks the soil down and wears it away, damaging the landscape.

★ Dry, dead plants can act as kindling which, when combined with high temperatures, can easily catch fire. Wildfires are a side effect of drought and are becoming an increasing problem around the world.

HABITAT HERO: RESSURECTION PLANT

Native to the Chihuahuan Desert in the USA and Mexico, this desert plant performs a miracle. It can survive years of drying out from extreme dehydration, then come back from the dead as soon as water finally returns.

While arid environments are perfectly natural, the increasing level of dryness caused by climate change is a problem. But don't worry, there are plenty of eco explorer activities that you can do to help your ecosystem in times of drought.

REUSE WATER

Using water more than once is a good habit. Place a bucket in the shower to catch excess water, called graywater, then use this to water your plants or flush the toilet.

DROUGHT-TOLERANT GARDENING

When selecting new plants, choose plants that can survive with little watering, such as lavender, succulents, rosemary, and sedums.

SWITCH OFF THE TAP

Fix leaky taps and always turn them off properly, especially when brushing your teeth. This will save lots of water in the long term.

DITCH THE WATER ACTIVITIES

During droughts, we need to prioritize water for important uses such as drinking, which means no water fights, filling up your pool, or using sprinklers.

THROW SOME MULCH AROUND

After an adult mows the lawn, throw all of the grass cuttings back onto the lawn and around your plants. This helps to retain moisture in the soil by adding shade and slowing down evaporation.

Adapting your behavior like this may take a bit of getting used to, but everything you do to reduce your water wastage will help to make a difference and potentially save lives.

ACTIVITY: BUILD A RAINWATER HARVESTER

Many of us take having water for granted as we have instant access to running water in our homes. However, that's not always a luxury found in arid ecosystems, so you'll want to collect as much water as you can. Luckily, there's a big source of free fresh water—rain!

RECYCLE YOUR WATER

While recycled rainwater is not suitable as drinking water, it can be used for plenty of other activities that require water in a drought, including watering plants, washing cars, and flushing the toilet.

COLLECT YOUR RAIN

You can collect rain with a rainwater harvester, a device that stores it for use when conditions become drier and water more scarce.

RAIN BARRELS

These are big, cylindrical tanks that connect to house gutters. Rain trickles from the roof into the gutters, then flows into the rain barrel, which has a little tap at the bottom for using the water later.

Rain barrels are a great option, but there are also mini rain harvesting devices that you can make at home by using just a few items of rubbish. So not only are you helping to conserve water, you're also recycling some of your plastic waste.

Eco Explorer Kit List:

- **Plastic bottle**
- **Sharp scissors**
- **Pebbles**
- **Ruler**
- **Permanent marker pen**

Step 1: Ask an adult to cut off the top quarter of your plastic bottle—watch out for any sharp edges!

Step 2: Place a handful of clean pebbles at the bottom of your bottle to stop it toppling over.

Step 3: Turn the cut off bottle top upside down and place it inside the rest of the bottle to create a funnel system for any rainwater you collect.

Step 4: Using the ruler and pen, mark points every centimeter up the length of your bottle to measure exactly how much rain you've collected.

Now put your plastic rainwater harvester outside and wait for the rain to come!

TOP TIP

The wider your bottle the more rain water it will catch. A large soda bottle or plastic milk carton is best.

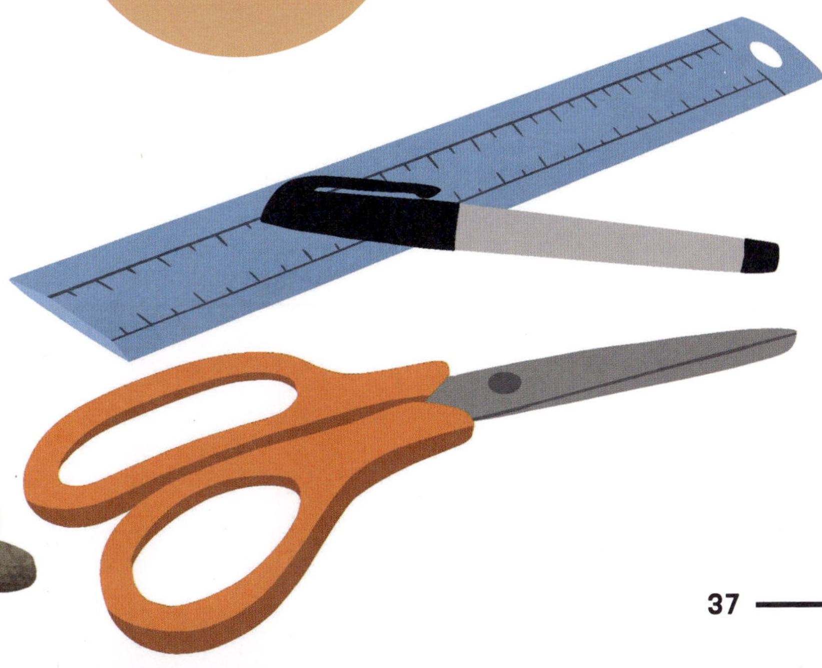

ACTIVITY: BUILD A TELESCOPE FOR STARGAZING

Rain comes from clouds, so one advantage of a dry environment is that there are often no clouds, which is perfect for night-time stargazing!

DID YOU KNOW

One of the closest stars to planet Earth is our very own sun, but even that is over 93 million miles away!

The universe contains billions of stars, a number too big for our brains to imagine. Some are hundreds of light years away and can only be seen with a powerful NASA telescope, while others are closer to home. Over 2,000 stars are visible in the night sky with just our eyes.

Humans have divided these visible stars into 88 different constellations, where groups of stars are joined together to make different shapes, a bit like a dot-to-dot picture.

The constellation Orion forms the shape of a hunter, Cassiopeia is the shape of a W and represents a woman sitting on her throne, and the Big Dipper looks a bit like a soup ladle.

Light pollution from street lamps and houses dims the natural brightness of the stars, making stargazing harder. You'll see more stars in an isolated and rural place than from your yard or window.

DID YOU KNOW

Space agencies such as NASA and ESA help us to learn about space. Their scientists build rockets that travel to distant moons and planets, as well as big telescopes that show us the universe.

ADVENTURE CHALLENGE

How many different constellations can you spot in the night sky? Can you make up any of your own?

To see the stars and constellations in more detail, you will need a telescope. Luckily, it's very easy to build your own with just a few materials found around the home.

★★★★★★★★★★★★★★★★★★★★★★★★★

HOW IT WORKS

The curved lenses in a telescope bend the light entering your eye, which makes the stars seem closer than they really are. It's important that you use convex lenses, like those from reading glasses, which are used to magnify text. Lenses used to correct long-sight won't work.

★★★★★★★★★★★★★★★★★★★★★★★★★

Eco Explorer Kit List:

- **Scissors**
- **2 paper towel tubes**
- **Biodegradable paper tape or masking tape**
- **Old reading glasses (ask an adult to carefully take out the lenses)**
- **Paint/colored pens**

Step 1: Cut one of your tubes all the way down one side to make the thinner inner tube of your telescope. Now slide that tube into the other one.

Step 2: Use tape to attach one lens to the bottom of the inner tube. Make sure the curved side of the lens is pointing into the tube.

Step 3: Attach the second lens to the opening of the outer tube. This time make sure the curved side is pointing away from the tube. Don't cover the lens with so much tape that you can't see through them.

Step 4: Now get creative and decorate the outside of your telescope using paints or pens.

All you need to do now is hold your telescope up to your eye, look through the lens of the inner tube, and slide that tube in and out until you can see the stars clearly. You've made a telescope that NASA would be proud of!

SAFETY FIRST:
Never use your telescope to look directly at the sun. It's extremely bright and can damage our eyes.

FRESHWATER

Without water, there would be no life on Earth. While oceans provide saltwater habitats, freshwater ones are also widespread around the globe and provide a home for a whole host of incredibly diverse living things.

DID YOU KNOW?

The largest freshwater source in the world is Lake Baikal in Siberia, which holds around 20% of all the unfrozen freshwater on Earth.

DID YOU KNOW?

Freshwater habitats around the world support over 17,000 species of fish and around 25,000 species of aquatic plants.

DID YOU KNOW?

Almost 70% of Earth's freshwater is stored as ice, mostly in the polar ice caps of Antarctica and Greenland.

ADVENTURE CHALLENGE

Go on a scavenger hunt to find a waterbird feather, a smooth pebble, a piece of driftwood, an empty snail shell, and an old dragonfly exoskeleton!

Freshwater habitats include everything from the mightiest of rivers and the deepest of lakes, to boggy wetlands and a small yard pond. They're one of the most important environments on the planet.

Not only do they sustain life both in and out of the water, they also provide land creatures, including us humans, with drinking water.

Aquatic life lives beneath the water surface while semi-aquatic creatures spend time both on land and in water. Other animals depend on freshwater for drinking and hunting, such as bats, who swoop over to chase hovering insects.

DID YOU KNOW?

The hard outer covering that some animals have to protect their soft bodies inside is called an exoskeleton. The empty exoskeleton left behind when a young dragonfly nymph transforms into an adult is called an exuvia.

Look Out For:

Can you spot these aquatic or semi-aquatic animals?

FISH
Freshwater habitats make perfect homes for fish as they provide them with food, shelter, and places to lay their eggs.

BIRD EGGS
Lots of water birds, such as swans and geese, make nests on the ground at the water's edge. Keep an eye out for nests, especially in the spring, but be careful not to disturb them.

CRAYFISH
Ocean-dwelling lobsters are related to crayfish, which can be found in freshwater rivers.

MAMMALS
Riverbanks are the perfect place for small, semi-aquatic mammals to make their home. See if you can spot creatures such as otters, beavers, rats, and water voles at your local river.

Freshwater habitats are carefully balanced ecosystems, but some human activities are upsetting that balance and putting aquatic life at risk. For example, when chemical fertilizers are used in farming and gardening but eventually make their way into a local freshwater habitat, it's called eutrophication.

★ BUILD-UP OF PLANT NUTRIENTS from fertilizers feeds tiny organisms called algae, which then multiply or bloom, turning the water green. This unfortunately blocks sunlight from getting into the water, reducing oxygen levels and leaving wildlife below the surface struggling to survive.

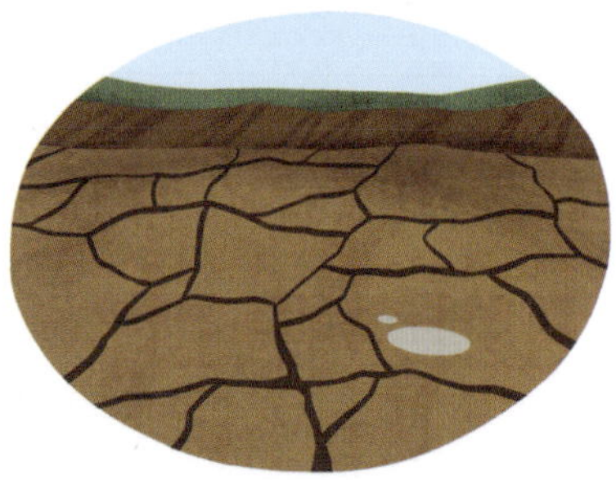

★ CLIMATE CHANGE is also affecting our freshwater habitats. Higher intensity droughts are causing rivers and lakes to completely dry up in some regions, starving the wildlife of their lifeline.

★ OVERFISHING occurs when too many fish are caught in a lake or river, causing a decline in fish numbers. This disrupts the food chain (every species that relies on fish for food will now go hungry) and can harm the entire ecosystem.

HABITAT HERO: POND SNAILS

While sometimes seen as a pest in a pond, snails should actually get a big thank you! Their favorite food is algae, which means they can fight the effects of eutrophication and keep ponds cleaner. This allows lots of other species to thrive there.

Eutrophication can be very harmful to aquatic ecosystems. Luckily, there are plenty of ways eco explorers can help to reverse this and save aquatic lives.

Encourage adults to stop using fertilizer in their yards. While their vegetables might not grow as big, or their flowers as pretty, the wildlife will benefit!

When choosing your fruit and vegetables at the supermarket, look for labels that say they've been grown using organic fertilizer. These are made from natural ingredients so they don't release as many harmful chemicals.

Try making your own homemade fertilizer with banana peel soaked in water for a few days, crushed eggshells, coffee grounds, or composting food scraps.

Plant a buffer zone of vegetation around your pond. These plants will act as a net to trap any fertilizer and stop it from reaching the water.

Hold your nose for this next suggestion, but you can ask local farmers if they have any animal manure to spread on your flowerbeds. This is a safe way to grow healthy plants.

ACTIVITY: GO POND DIPPING

Ponds are the most common freshwater habitat and there are probably hundreds of millions of them around the world. You might have a pond already, but if not, then turn to page 14 to find out how to build one.

You'll find lots of interesting invertebrates, amphibians and plant life in a pond. Here's a fun way to say hello to them.

A great way to really see what's in a pond is to grab a net and go pond dipping. You could also build the bathyscope on page 23 to spy beneath the water's surface without disturbing the creatures there.

Eco Explorer Kit List:

- **Waterproof boots**
- **Plastic container such as a bucket or tub**
- **Net**
- **Magnifying glass**
- **Pencil and notepad**

Step 1: Before you get started, put on your waterproof boots. With help from an adult, dunk your plastic container into the pond and scoop up some water as a temporary habitat for any aquatic creatures you find.

Step 2: Dip your net into the pond water and sweep it gently around to avoid damaging any of the plants.

Step 3: Now see what you've caught. Remove your net from the water, turn it inside out and carefully shake out the contents into your container filled with water.

SAFETY FIRST:

Always be careful around open water and go with an adult as it can be a lot deeper than it looks –and never get too close to the edge!

Step 4: If you're lucky, you'll see lots of different creatures. Use your magnifying glass to get a close-up look at them.

Step 5: Use your pencil and notepad to write down or draw all the species you've found. Compare these with your next pond dip.

Pond dipping is a bit like a nature treasure hunt. How many different types of aquatic life can you find?

TOP TIP 1

Spring and summer are the best seasons to do a pond dip, as this is when most creatures will be around.

TOP TIP 2

Dip your net at different depths. A deep-water sweep will give you different critters to sweeps nearer to the surface of the water.

ACTIVITY: MAKE A NATURE SCULPTURE

Ever since the beginning of humankind, art has been inspired by nature—from ancient cave paintings of bison to Van Gogh's sunflowers. Natural environments offer a mix of colors, patterns, and textures and are proven to calm our brains. No wonder they've been so influential!

Not only can art be inspired by nature, it can also be made out of nature! Objects like pine cones and flower petals are excellent materials to make into creative artwork.

Because freshwater habitats are so diverse, they are great places to hunt for nature materials. Go explore your local freshwater habitat and the surrounding areas to forage for interesting materials, then have a go at making your own nature sculptures.

There's no right or wrong way to make a nature sculpture—just be as creative as possible and see where your imagination takes you.

Think about things you've seen in nature that you can recreate with the natural materials you find. Use glue, string, or tape to attach all your materials together as you build your sculpture. You could even add paint or eco glitter to decorate it.

Eco Explorer Kit List:

- **Natural materials such as pine cones, leaves, conkers, rocks, twigs, and petals**
- **Scissors**
- **Glue, string, and tape**
- **Paint and eco glitter**
- **Extra craft supplies, such as pipe cleaners or googly eyes (optional)**

Here are some ideas to get you started:

★ A pine cone bird with leaves for the tail, wings, and feet.

★ A spider made out of a conker using pipe cleaners for legs.

★ A rock painted to look like a ladybug.

★ A butterfly with a short twig for the body and flower petals as the wings.

★ Leaves wrapped around a twisty twig to make a snake.

With some creativity, you'll soon have loads of impressive sculptures to put on display.

In modern society, nature has also inspired some of our advanced engineering projects. For example, when Japan built their high-speed bullet trains, they found that the trains made a loud booming sound when leaving a tunnel.

Luckily, nature helped solve this problem. The engineers saw how a kingfisher's streamlined beak helped it dive into water more smoothly. When they designed a pointy nose for their trains it helped to make them quieter.

COLD CLIMATES

Cold environments aren't easy to live in. Temperatures can drop below freezing and there's little vegetation to eat. Despite this, they are still a vital ecosystem and habitat for many extraordinary species that have adapted to deal with the cold.

DID YOU KNOW?
Polar bears have black skin under their white fur because it's the best color to absorb heat from the sun.

DID YOU KNOW?
Elephant seals have a thick layer of fat called blubber that keeps them warm.

DID YOU KNOW?
Arctic foxes are one of many cold-climate animals that have smaller ears because big ears lose heat quicker.

All these things contribute to a habitat being cold:

LATITUDE
Latitude is how far away a place is from the equator. The areas furthest from the equator and closer to the north and south poles experience much less heat from the sun.

ALTITUDE
Altitude is the height above sea level. The higher the altitude, the less atmosphere there is to trap heat.

SEASON
In many places, winter months are the coldest because Earth is tilted so the sunlight there is less intense.

DID YOU KNOW?
The Arctic woolly bear moth caterpillar can freeze completely solid during winter, thawing out again in the spring.

DID YOU KNOW?

The coldest temperature ever recorded on Earth was -128.56 °F in East Antarctica.

ADVENTURE CHALLENGE

Many different animals leave tracks behind in the snow. How many different footprints can you spot?

- Deer: look for heart-shaped tracks left behind by their hooves.
- Dog and cat: look for a central pad surrounded by four toes—with visible claw marks for dogs, too.

DID YOU KNOW?

Snowshoe hares have massive feet to spread their body weight and stop them sinking into the soft snow.

- Squirrel: look for tiny versions of human handprints.
- Small rodent: look for small dots in the snow.

Look Out For:

Can you spot these cold climate animals?

HIBERNATING MAMMALS
Many mammals such as hedgehogs, bats, bears, and groundhogs enter a deep, sleep-like state called hibernation in winter. They use burrows, caves, or nests, so be careful not to disturb them.

HUNGRY BIRDS
Food is scarce during the winter months, so don't be surprised if you see the odd hungry bird landing in your yard to forage for food.

GRAY SEALS
If you live near the coast, you might see female gray seals come onto the beach to give birth and rear their pups during the early winter months when its cold.

SQUIRRELS
You might spot these rodents burying secret stashes of nuts and seeds in the fall, or returning to eat them in winter when other food sources are low. This is called caching.

The biggest threat that cold climate habitats currently face is climate change. With temperatures around the world increasing, and the Arctic warming at about twice the rate of the global average, these habitats are in trouble.

DID YOU KNOW?
In some places climate change is actually making winters harsher, leaving the wildlife that lives there struggling to adapt.

WARMING TEMPERATURES cause ice sheets to melt, glaciers to shrink and permafrost to thaw out, so the icy habitats get smaller and smaller for the local wildlife.

All that melted ice also produces huge volumes of water. With nowhere else to go, the water ends up in the ocean, causing sea levels to rise. This leads to flooding in coastal areas worldwide.

Because ice is white, it reflects a lot of the sun's rays back out to space in a process known as albedo. Less ice means less sunlight is reflected, so Earth heats up even more—it's a vicious cycle.

HABITAT HERO: ANTARCTIC NOTOTHENIOID FISH

[Pronunciation: no-to-ten-ee-oid]

This peculiar group of fish live in the waters surrounding Antarctica and have an unusual way of surviving the cold. Special substances in their blood bind to ice crystals to stop them from freezing.

Reducing climate change is a huge task that nobody can solve alone, but it's down to us eco explorers to give a helping hand to the wildlife suffering as the winter months get colder and harsher in many parts of the world.

HYDRATE THE ANIMALS

The freshwater sources that animals drink from often freeze in winter. Try smashing any ice that forms or float an empty plastic bottle in the water to stop ice from forming.

FEED THE ANIMALS

Food is scarcer in winter so put out seeds and fruit for birds, nuts for squirrels, cooked meat for foxes, and dog food for hedgehogs. Avoid harmful salty foods, junk food, bread, or milk.

CHECK YOUR BONFIRES

Making a bonfire is a fun way to keep warm in the winter, but many animals, such as hedgehogs, frogs, and mice, keep themselves cozy in piles of logs. Always check your bonfires before an adult lights them.

DON'T PRUNE THE SHRUBS

Shrubbery provides a safe home for many insects to live in during the winter, so make sure you remind any adults of this if they want to prune the shrubs.

DON'T OVER-TIDY YOUR YARD

Leaving piles of leaf litter or fallen branches in your yard can help many animals who might use them for shelter and even to hibernate in. So it's important that you don't pick them up, even if it makes your yard look a little untidy.

ACTIVITY: COOK A CALORIE CAKE FOR THE BIRDS

Measured in a unit called calories, food gives us energy that our bodies use in lots of different ways. Birds use this energy when they forage, build nests, fly, sing, and also to maintain their temperature. Because of this, they need plenty of food. However, in winter, this food is much harder to find.

Making a calorie cake for your local birds ensures they have access to enough food to keep them flying and singing everyday.

Birds really struggle in the winter, but you can help them out. Fat-rich foods will provide them with lots of precious energy, but adding nuts and seeds will give them a more balanced diet. So let's get cooking!

Eco Explorer Kit List:

- **Half a coconut shell (or empty yogurt pot)**
- **Twine**
- **Fat, such as suet or lard**
- **Saucepan**
- **Wooden spoon**
- **Dry ingredients: nuts, seeds, dried insects, fresh berries, or dried fruit**
- **Mixing bowl**

Step 1: Ask an adult to poke a hole into the edge of the coconut shell and tie a piece of twine through it.

Step 2: Next, ask an adult to melt the fat in the pan, then carefully stir it into your dry ingredients in a bowl. You'll need about half as much fat as dry ingredients.

Step 3: Spoon the mixture into the coconut shell until it's completely full. Make sure it's packed in well.

Step 4: Set your calorie cake in the fridge overnight, then hang it outside the next day.

SAFETY FIRST:
Always ask an adult to help you with anything that needs heating, cutting, or drilling.

Vary your ingredients to attract different birds:

★ Dried mealworms for tits
★ Berries for finches and robins
★ Chopped apple for blackbirds
★ Grated cheese for wrens
★ Nyjer seeds for sparrows
★ Unsalted peanuts for starlings

Most birds will eat almost anything, so don't be surprised if your tasty creations attract a wide range of species.

ACTIVITY: BUILD A HIBERNACULUM

With cold temperatures, scarce food, and frozen water, many animals require more energy than they can get from food in winter. To survive, some migrate to warmer places, but others hibernate, sleeping right through winter until the warmer spring.

Some animals enter a state of dormancy in the winter, which changes the animal's body to reduce energy consumption. This is called hibernation.

- To make it through hibernation, it's important that the animal first eats as much as possible to build up its energy-storing fat reserves.
- Their body temperature lowers to try to match the outside temperature.
- Their heart rate decreases and their breathing slows down. They enter a sleep-like state so they don't waste any energy moving around.

Lots of animals hibernate, from bears, ladybugs, and hamsters, to frogs, bats, and snakes. For reptiles and amphibians, the process is called brumation, while other animals can switch in and out of hibernation in a state called torpor.

DID YOU KNOW?

During hibernation, a hedgehog's heart rate drops from 190 to 20 beats per minute to conserve energy.

All hibernating animals need a safe place to hibernate, sheltered from the elements. A hibernaculum is a great structure to build outside to give wildlife a place to shelter during the winter. This one is particularly good for reptiles and amphibians.

Eco Explorer Kit List:

- **Spade**
- **3-4 drainpipe pieces about 32 inches long**
- **Rocks, logs, bricks, sticks, broken slabs, tiles, and plant pots**
- **Fallen leaves**
- **Wildflower seeds**

Step 1: Ask an adult to dig a hole roughly 20 inches deep and 60 inches wide somewhere outside that drains easily when it rains.

Step 2: Place the drainpipes in the hole, making sure one end of each sits above ground as an entrance.

Step 3: Fill in the hole with objects such as rocks, logs, bricks, sticks, broken slabs, tiles, and plant pots. Leave plenty of gaps to make animal passageways.

TOP TIP

Place a stick down each drain pipe to give animals something to grip onto when they crawl through.

Step 4: Now cover these materials in a thick layer of fallen leaves to trap in heat.

Step 5: Cover everything except for the drainpipe entrances with a mound of the dug out soil. This will insulate the hibernaculum and protect it from the weather outside.

Step 6: Scatter wildflower seeds on the soil. Flowers will have the added bonus of attracting pollinators.

Now wait until winter and hopefully some guests will slither or hop into your cozy hibernaculum.

UNDERGROUND

One habitat that's often overlooked is right below our feet—underground! There's an entire world living in the soil beneath us, filled with critters, microscopic life, bacteria, and fungi.

DID YOU KNOW?

Cicada nymphs can spend up to 17 years underground, before living for just a few weeks above ground as an adult insect.

ADVENTURE CHALLENGE

Dig a hole in the ground. How many creatures can you find in the soil you've taken out?

Lots of different animals can be found underground. Mammals such as moles tunnel through soil, while ants build huge empires to store food and rear their young. Birds such as burrowing owls and puffins dig burrows to build nests inside the soil.

Perhaps the most iconic underground creature is the earthworm. It is one of the most important animals on the planet. Earthworms create tunnels that let air into the soil, help water to flow, spread nutrients, and regulate the pH level.

Creatures choose a soil habitat for various reasons:

TEMPERATURE REGULATION

Soil acts as an insulator, so temperatures inside it don't change as much as above ground.

PROTECTION

Soil provides a natural barrier from predators and the wind, rain, ice, and snow.

FOOD ABUNDANCE

Soil contains things like decaying leaves and rotting wood—a detritivorous, soil-living creature is literally surrounded by food.

WATER SOURCE

Soil holds moisture well, so it can provide constant hydration for the animals living there.

DID YOU KNOW?

An average yard contains about 20 earthworms per square foot of soil!

DID YOU KNOW?

Earthworms have both male and female reproductive organs. This means they are called hermaphrodites.

Look Out For:

Can you spot these underground animals?

EARTHWORM CASTINGS
Look out for tiny mounds of soil on your lawn, no bigger than a few millimeters long. These are actually earthworm poops, or "castings", which help fertilize the soil.

CREEPY-CRAWLIES
Many other critters spend time underground, too. Keep an eye out for beetles, centipedes, woodlice, and earwigs.

HUNGRY BIRDS
When it rains, earthworms come to the surface to avoid drowning. Some birds have learned to tap their feet on the ground to mimic rainfall, then gobble any worms that pop up!

Soil is absolutely vital in Earth's ecosystems. As well as housing many living things, it filters drinking water and stores lots of carbon dioxide that would otherwise be released into the atmosphere. Sadly, humans often cause harm to these diverse underground habitats. Here are two key examples.

★ OVERUSING CHEMICAL PESTICIDES in our yards and on our farmland can cause contamination to the soil, stripping out the natural nutrients and polluting it with harmful substances.

While chemical pesticides should target a specific pest species, they often harm others, too. This has a knock-on effect further up the food chain and can cause huge biodiversity loss in the entire ecosystem.

★ WHEN FORESTS ARE CLEARED during deforestation, the soil loses its vegetation cover. It becomes a lot more exposed to the elements, and wind and water can now erode it more easily, making it gradually wear away.

HABITAT HERO: DUNG BEETLES

There are lots of detritivores that will happily break down rotting plant waste, but not many of them are as keen to devour animal poop. Luckily, dung beetles love the stuff!

Pesticide use threatens the survival of many insects and other invertebrates that are crucial for a successful ecosystem. But pesticide damage is something humans can control—we just have to stop using them.

Understandably, nobody wants pests on their vegetable patch, munching away on their plants and crops. Luckily, there are plenty of chemical-free alternatives to using pesticides—and it's up to you as an eco explorer to encourage people to use them.

ENCOURAGE NATURAL PREDATORS

Frogs love to eat slugs, so building a pond to tempt them will help to reduce your slug population. Also, letting stinging nettles grow will encourage ladybugs, who will munch on any annoying aphids.

COMPANION PLANTING

Strong-smelling plants like marigolds, garlic, or mint will repel pests. Or place extra plants, such as lettuces, around a vegetable patch so they eat those instead.

PHYSICAL BARRIERS

Covering your much-loved plants with mesh netting will help to protect them from larger animals like birds or rabbits.

NATURAL PESTICIDES

To deter pests without harming the environment, scatter crushed eggshells or coffee grounds, or place beer traps and copper coins on the ground.

ACTIVITY: GET COMPOSTING

Just like every other animal, we humans produce organic waste—and not just poop! Things like the peel from a banana we've eaten get broken down by organisms called decomposers, such as the earthworm. They turn these waste materials into a nutritious mixture that we call compost.

DID YOU KNOW?

When microorganisms turn waste into compost it produces enough heat to make a compost heap up to 122°F inside.

You only need three simple ingredients for successful composting: waste, air, and water.

Making compost is a great way to live more sustainably and become a brilliant eco explorer. This is how it helps:

REDUCES NEED FOR CHEMICAL FERTILIZERS

Compost is packed full of all the nutrients soil needs to grow healthy, strong plants.

REDUCES LANDFILL

By composting, you'll have less waste to send to landfill, which helps to reduce the damage caused by landfill.

PROVIDES HABITATS

A warm compost heap attracts hungry minibeasts who eat the waste, and small mammals and reptiles seeking a cozy place to rest.

Composting is a natural process and all organic waste will break down eventually. The bigger the container, the more compost you'll be able to make, but even using a plastic bottle would work.

There are two types of composting ingredients to add to your bin: brown and green. Brown materials contain lots of carbon, whereas green materials have more nitrogen. Both are important nutrients so aim for a 50/50 mix.

Eco Explorer Kit List:

- **Cordless drill**
- **Plastic container with a lid, such as a trash can**
- **Compostable ingredients**
- **Shovel, trowel, or an old fork**
- **Watering can**

Step 1: Ask an adult to drill holes in the bottom of your container. These will allow excess moisture to drain out and let more decomposers and oxygen in.

Step 2: Put your composting ingredients into the container (half green and half brown!), then place your compost bin in a shady spot outside.

Step 3: Use a shovel, trowel, or fork to turn over the contents of the bin once a month. This lets more air in and helps the decomposers do their job.

Step 4: Occasionally add water to your compost bin to keep it damp but not waterlogged. You can add more waste when there's room, too.

It can take a few months for your bin to start producing compost. It's ready to use when the mixture is dark and crumbly and smells more like earth than rotting vegetables.

WHAT CAN AND CAN'T GO ON THE COMPOST HEAP?

Green materials:
- ✔ **Vegetable peel**
- ✔ **Grass cuttings**
- ✔ **Dead leaves**
- ✔ **Coffee grounds**

Brown materials:
- ✔ **Eggshells**
- ✔ **Newspapers**
- ✔ **Sawdust pet bedding**

- ✘ **Cooked food scraps**
- ✘ **Woody stems**
- ✘ **Meat**
- ✘ **Carnivore poop**
- ✘ **Diseased plants**
- ✘ **Weed seedheads**

ACTIVITY: BUILD A WORMERY

Decomposers such as earthworms break down organic waste and recycle nutrients from it back into the environment. They're like nature's rubbish collectors and an extremely important part of an underground ecosystem.

Building a wormery allows you to have your very own slice of the underground in your house. It lets you watch how earthworms tunnel through the soil, mixing it all up and slowly decomposing any dead leaves or food scraps you put on the surface.

DID YOU KNOW?

There are over 6,000 different species of earthworm around the world, so the ones you find for your wormery will depend on where you live. But they all do a great job of decomposing.

TOP TIP

While you can dig up some soil to find your earthworms, it's much easier to leave a wet piece of cardboard on the ground overnight. You should find plenty of worms sitting under it the next morning.

There are lots of different types of wormery that you can buy, but the best thing to do is to make your own. All you need to make one is a few household items—and some earthworms!

Eco Explorer Kit List:

- **2 litre clear plastic bottle**
- **Scissors**
- **Soil, compost, and sand**
- **Earthworms**
- **Fallen leaves**
- **Jug of water**
- **Compostable plastic wrap**
- **Rubber band or string**
- **1 sheet of newspaper**
- **Biodegradable paper tape**

Step 1: Remove any labels from your plastic bottle and ask an adult to cut off the top third.

Step 2: Build up layers of soil, compost, and sand in the bottle. These layers won't be as obvious once your earthworms get to work.

Step 3: Add the earthworms—around three or four—to your plastic bottle.

Step 4: Scatter some fallen leaves on the top for the earthworms to eat. Sprinkle some water in to keep it damp.

Step 5: Secure some plastic wrap over the top of your bottle with a rubber band—this will stop the earthworms escaping. Ask an adult to pierce a few tiny holes in the bottle so the worms can breathe.

TOP TIP

Be gentle when handling earthworms and don't leave them out of soil for too long.

Step 6: Earthworms like the dark, so wrap the bottle with a piece of newspaper secured with tape. You can remove this whenever you want to peek inside.

To keep your worms happy you need to remember to do two things: keep your wormery in a cool, sheltered place and top up the dead leaves and water.

IN THE CITY

As the human population increases, we will need more places to live. Many people choose to move to urban environments, so every year current cities are expanded and new ones are built. This is called urbanization.

DID YOU KNOW?

Over 56% of humans live in cities now, and it could be as many as 70% of us by 2050.

DID YOU KNOW?

Cities can often be around 53.6°F warmer than surrounding rural areas.

ADVENTURE CHALLENGE

Grab your binoculars, a notepad, and a pencil, and go on a city wildlife safari with an adult. Jot down what you see!

In the long history of life on Earth, urban environments are a fairly new habitat. Although urbanization is causing vast habitat loss and puts many species at risk, others have successfully adapted to city life. Many species actually thrive thanks to all the places to shelter and constant food sources in a city.

However, with more and more of us now living in cities, people are becoming increasingly disconnected from nature.

That being said, there are plenty of opportunities to interact with nature in a city, so it's your mission as an eco explorer to educate people about the importance of reconnecting and interacting positively with nature, wherever they live.

DID YOU KNOW?

There are around 10,000 cities in the world. The largest is Tokyo in Japan, home to 37.5 million people!

Look Out For:

Can you spot these city animals?

BIRDS OF PREY

Cities provide a variety of small rodents for birds of prey to eat. They also have tall buildings, such as cathedrals and skyscrapers, to replace their natural nesting sites on high rocks.

SCAVENGERS

Thanks to all the food waste left by us humans, cities provide a feast for many scavenging animals. These include foxes, raccoons, and even bears, though it depends on where you are in the world.

PIGEONS

The birds that have adapted best to living in the city are pigeons. They can be found in huge numbers in cities all over the world.

BATS

Some bat species love cities because there are plenty of insects for them to feed on, drawn in by the bright city lights. Bats also love the slightly warmer temperatures in cities.

Not all species have adapted to life in cities, which are built mostly with humans in mind. Even the animals that have adapted well are still threatened by living so closely to people.

★ HABITAT LOSS AND FRAGMENTATION

As cities grow, more natural habitats are lost or broken up by walls and fences. Animals forced into city life can struggle to find food, mates, and shelter.

★ POLLUTION

Cities are loud places that are more heavily polluted than the countryside. There are more cars, traffic, and things like factories emitting greenhouse gases. All this noise and air pollution can cause animals stress and harm.

★ LIGHT POLLUTION

Bright city lights can also disrupt wildlife. For example, street lights weaken the glows of a glow-worm. As males struggle to spot the glowing females to mate, the species declines.

★ DOMESTIC ANIMALS

More people also means more pets, and some domestic animals, like cats, can cause lots of harm to local wildlife. Outdoor cats hunt billions of birds and small mammals every year.

HABITAT HERO: CANADA GEESE

Originally native to the temperate regions of North America, highly intelligent Canada geese have adapted well to city environments. In urban areas all over the world, they help to disperse plants by pooping out their seeds.

With so many threats to wildlife in cities, and more and more creatures being forced there by urbanization, it can seem like a losing battle. But eco explorers don't give up easily! Here are some things you can do to help.

BUILD NATURE CORRIDORS

Ask an adult to cut a hole about 5.5 x 5.5 inches at the bottom of your fence. This opening, or "nature corridor", will help small creatures like frogs and hedgehogs to find food, mates, and territory more easily.

SWITCH OFF THE LIGHTS

Reduce the amount of outdoor lighting you use. Either switch off your outdoor lights or use sensors so that they only come on if someone goes outside.

CONTROL YOUR CATS

Keep your pet cats indoors or attach a bell to their collar to scare off any small animals before they have a chance to catch them.

WRITE TO YOUR LOCAL AUTHORITY

Write a letter to your local council to ask them to develop more green spaces for wildlife. One idea to propose is to plant wildflowers on grass verges around town to attract pollinating insects.

GET YOUR CLASSMATES INVOLVED

Recruit more eco explorers by encouraging your school to plant wildflowers in the playground. You could even ask your teachers if they could build a nature pond there.

ACTIVITY: MAKE WILDFLOWER SEED BOMBS

Cities are busy environments, often with very little free space available. It's important that we make the most of every single bit there is, no matter how small. A simple way of doing this is by planting wildflowers.

Wildflowers attract a wide range of insects, including pollinators. They can grow in relatively nutrient-poor soils, so are perfect for growing in cities. If you don't have a yard, grow wildflowers in a window box or create a community patch with your neighbors. Mixed wildflower seed packets will vary depending on where you live, but here are some common species:

You could simply scatter your wildflower seeds on the soil for them to grow, but making wildflower seed bombs is a lot more fun and can help you to grow flowers in places that are harder to reach.

The amount of compost and flour doesn't need to be precise. Make sure to use the same cup or mug (it can be any size) and measure about 5 cups of compost and 2 cups of flour.

Eco Explorer Kit List:

- **Measuring cups**
- **5 cups of compost**
- **2 cups of flour**
- **Mixing bowl**
- **Packet of wildflower seeds**
- **Water**
- **Paprika (optional)**

Step 1: Place your compost and flour into your mixing bowl, then add all the seeds from the packet.

Step 2: Mix the ingredients together with your hands. Slowly add more and more water to the mix until it becomes a sticky dough.

Step 3: Roll your dough into the size of golf balls, then leave them to dry overnight. You could even get creative and mold them into different shapes.

TOP TIP 2

Add a pinch of paprika to your mixture to stop birds eating the seeds—it will put them off without harming them.

TOP TIP 1

Check the back of the seed packet to find the best time of year to sow your particular type of wildflowers.

Step 4: Throw your seed bombs outside, wherever you want wildflowers to grow. They should explode as they land, scattering lots of seeds around.

Make sure you water your seeds regularly and you should have a beautiful mini wildflower meadow teeming with pollinators in no time!

ACTIVITY: GO FORAGING

With most of us getting our food from grocery stores, it's sometimes easy to forget that nature can provide us with plenty of things to eat. Loads of edible plants, berries, and fungi grow in the wild. Gathering wild food is called foraging. You can forage for some great things in a city. Head to a local green space with an adult and see what you can find.

Crab apples are a bit smaller than normal apples and taste quite sour raw, but are lovely cooked in jams, pies, and crumbles.

Elderberries grow in clusters of small, dark purple berries. They can upset your tummy when eaten raw, so always cook them first.

Chicken of the woods is an orange mushroom that grows in clusters up tree trunks and must be cooked before eating.

Wild garlic has broad leaves and small, star-shaped white flowers, which add the same garlic taste and smell to food.

Chanterelle mushrooms are bright yellowy-orange with white flesh when you cut into them. Always cook them before eating.

Blackberries are made up of tiny balls called drupelets and turn from red to deep purple-black when they're ripe.

SAFETY FIRST: There are some highly poisonous plants, mushrooms, and berries growing in the wild, and some are easy to confuse with edible ones. Always take an adult foraging with you and NEVER eat anything you are not 100% sure is safe.

All you need to go foraging is to get outdoors and see what you can find. You don't need any special equipment. Try to explore different microhabitats —you'll often find mushrooms in dark, damp spots closer to the ground and berries higher up in the shrubbery.

Eco Explorer Kit List:

- **Collecting basket**
- **Mushroom and plant identification books**
- **Sturdy footwear**

Here are a few things to keep in mind:

★ Using identification books and online resources will not only tell you if plants, berries, and mushrooms are safe to eat, but also where to look and clues to find them.

★ You'll find different forages depending on the month. A variety of mushrooms grow throughout the year, but edible plants and berries are most common around spring and summer.

★ Always wash what you find and forage from areas away from roadsides and places that haven't been treated with pesticides or other chemicals.

★ Be patient—you might not find what you're looking for every time but it's sometimes exciting to discover new things you didn't expect to see.

A little bit of foraging can provide some tasty treats, but make sure you forage sustainably. Take little bits from different areas, and no more than you can eat. This prevents over-harvesting and a loss in biodiversity.

GRASSLANDS

Grasslands are one of the most widespread habitats on Earth and are found on every continent except Antarctica. They cover up to 40% of all land on the planet so they are responsible for supporting large amounts of biodiversity.

A grassland is typically an open space where grasses, herbs, and wildflowers grow and there are no, or very few, trees. Grasses, such as wheat, barley, and corn, play a vital role in the ecosystem. They help stabilize the soil, offer shelter, and provide food for grazing animals and humans alike.

Grasslands include the well-known Great Plains of North America and the savannahs of the African Serengeti, but the grassland habitats we see more regularly are on a much smaller scale—in gardens, parks, and other local green spaces.

There are two main types of grassland habitats:

TEMPERATE GRASSLANDS are found in regions with moderate rainfall throughout the year. They include the prairies in North America, steppes in Eurasia, and pampas in South America.

TROPICAL GRASSLANDS are found nearer to the equator. They have distinctive wet and dry seasons and are also called savannahs.

DID YOU KNOW?
Kentucky bluegrass is one of the most common grasses used for lawns, sports fields, and parks worldwide.

DID YOU KNOW?
Pollinating insects play a vital role in maintaining grasslands. By pollinating flowers they help even more to grow.

ADVENTURE CHALLENGE

How many types of grazing animals can you name? Don't forget those in different parts of the world to you.

Look Out For:

Can you spot these grassland animals?

POLLINATORS
A healthy grassland often contains wildflowers of some sort, and these are an absolute haven for pollinating insects. Look out for bees, butterflies, beetles, and hoverflies.

GRAZERS
Grazing animals love eating grass, so they're naturally drawn to grasslands. Depending on where you live, you might spot sheep, bison, zebras, and even kangaroos munching away.

PREDATORS
With all the grazing animals around, grasslands also attract predators looking for a snack. They could be as big as a lion or wolf, or smaller like a fox or badger.

REPTILES
Lots of snake, lizard, and tortoise species love living in grasslands, where they can take advantage of the open space and plentiful plants, as well as insects and small rodents to eat.

Grasslands can support a lot of biodiversity, as well as provide us humans with valuable resources, such as food and leisure space. However, as with all habitats where humans and wildlife coexist, there can be conflict.

★ POORLY MANAGED FARMING is one of the many threats to grasslands. When you grow only one type of crop, this is called monoculture. It reduces biodiversity, degrades the soil, and encourages pests and crop disease. Also, if you allow livestock animals to overgraze the grasslands they live on, this can remove some plant species and compact the soil.

★ UNSUSTAINABLE GARDENING PRACTICES
Homeowners and local authorities tend to cut grass very short to look more appealing, but this doesn't help the wild flowers and animals that rely on them to survive.

★ ALIEN INVASIONS
Invasive plants and animals from other parts of the world are known as alien species, and sometimes they find their way into grassland ecosystems. They can cause harm by spreading diseases and taking food and shelter from native species.

HABITAT HERO: MASON BEES

Solitary bees such as mason bees are 120 times better at pollinating than the honeybee. Unlike honeybees, they don't have pollen baskets, so they drop a lot of pollen as they fly from flower to flower —pollinating them in the process.

With all these threats, grassland wildlife has suffered massive losses and the number of pollinating insects has decreased dramatically worldwide. But this just gives us eco explorers another mission—to reverse these impacts and make our grasslands flourish once again.

WRITE TO YOUR LOCAL AUTHORITY

Ask local authorities to mow the grass verges around town less often. This will allow grasses time to attract pollinators. Not killing the weeds helps, too, as they boost biodiversity and prevent monoculture.

PLANT NATIVE SPECIES

Species that are native to the local area will support wildlife and restore natural habitats, so plant more of these.

PRUNE NON-NATIVE SPECIES

If you're 100% certain plants are non-native, prune or remove them to give native plants a better chance of survival.

LEAVE A WILD PATCH

Leaving a section of your green space wild, with no mowing or pruning, will allow grasses and flowers to grow, attracting lots of pollinating insects and the larger animals that feast on them.

ACTIVITY: CONSTRUCT A POOTER

It's time to grab your magnifying glass and get close to some of our creepy-crawly friends. As grassland habitats are home to lots of native wildflower plants, they're the perfect place to go on a bug hunt.

There are over one million known insect species worldwide, and probably millions more that we haven't discovered yet. The ones you find on your bug hunt will depend on where you live, but here are some groups of bugs you'll almost certainly come across.

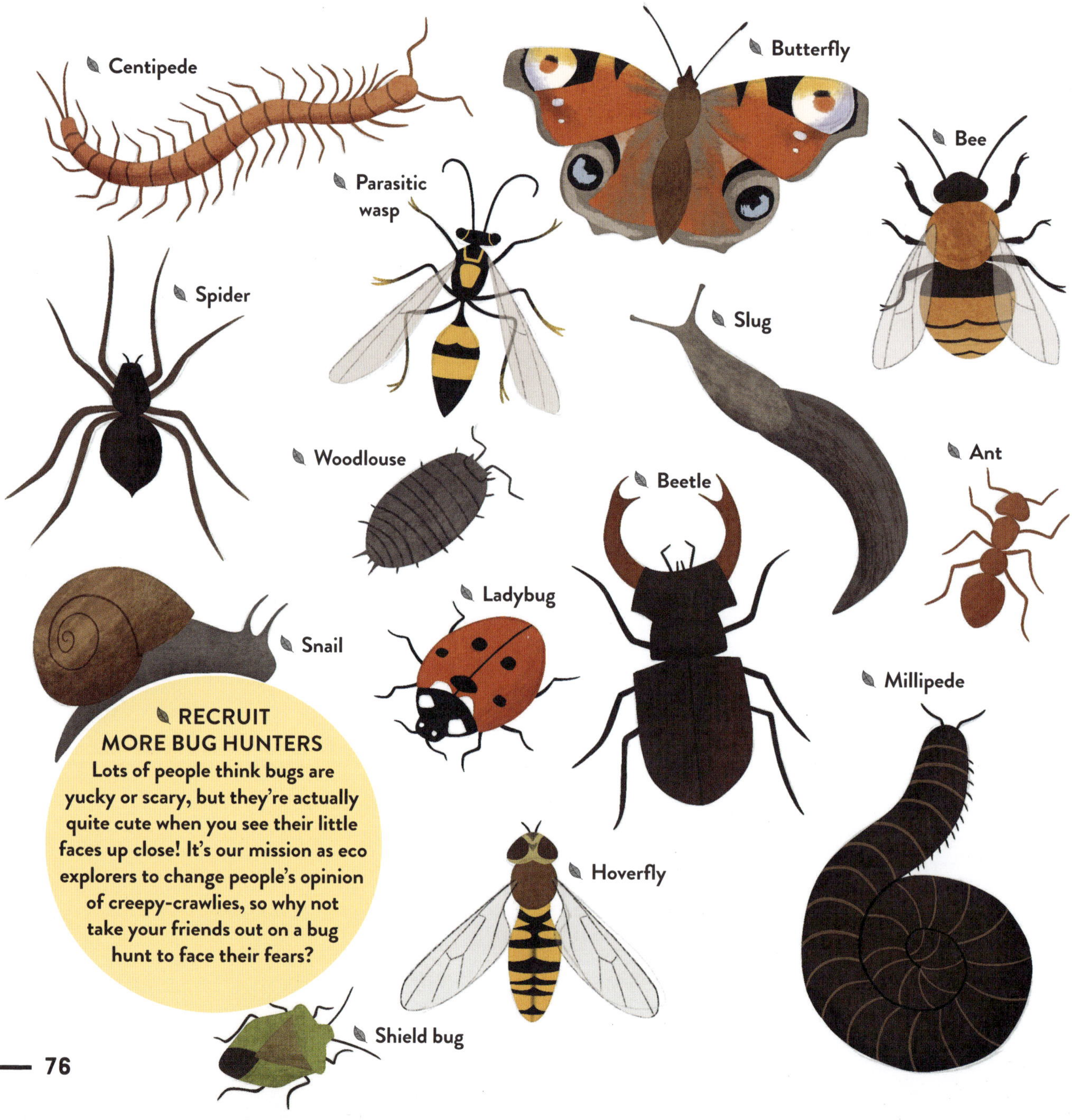

RECRUIT MORE BUG HUNTERS

Lots of people think bugs are yucky or scary, but they're actually quite cute when you see their little faces up close! It's our mission as eco explorers to change people's opinion of creepy-crawlies, so why not take your friends out on a bug hunt to face their fears?

It can be a bit tricky to catch bugs as many are very small and very fast—and some can even fly. Luckily, you can build something called a pooter to help you catch them. You don't need to touch the bugs; you can simply suck them up harmlessly into your pooter.

TOP TIP

Search for bugs in different places. What can you find on the ground compared to higher up on the grasses?

Eco Explorer Kit List:

- **Sharp scissors**
- **Small clear jar with a lid**
- **3 x 2 inch scrap of cloth**
- **2 bendy straws**
- **Rubber band or string**
- **Eco-friendly modelling clay**
- **Notepad and pencil**
- **Magnifying glass**

Step 1: Ask an adult to poke two straw-sized holes in the lid of your jar.

Step 2: Wrap the cloth around the bottom of one straw, keeping it in place with the rubber band. This will prevent you from sucking any bugs straight into your mouth!

Step 3: Push that straw through one of the holes in your lid, making sure the cloth end is inside the jar. Then push the other straw through the second hole.

Step 4: Squish your modelling clay into any gaps around both of the holes in the lid to make it as airtight as possible.

Step 5: Place your pooter on the ground and gently suck up air through the straw with the cloth tied to the end. Then watch as bugs travel up the other straw and into the container, ready to be inspected.

Now you've got your very own bug-collector! Use a magnifying glass to look at the tiny creatures you've collected while they're in your pooter—you could even draw them. But remember to release them back into the wild once you've had a good look.

ACTIVITY: MAKE A BOTANICAL SCRAPBOOK

Grassland habitats are full of beautiful wildflowers, grasses and seedheads, making them the perfect location to inspire this activity. A great way to become a budding botanist is to create your very own botanical scrapbook.

There really are no rules when choosing what to include—just head outdoors and look for plants that interest you, from striking flowers to tall grasses. With over 450,000 known plant species worldwide, the ones you find will definitely vary, but here are some common ones to look out for

SUSTAINABLE BOTANY: When collecting plants, only take a few from one area and only pick flowers that are plentiful. Some plants are extremely rare, so avoid damaging them when carrying out your botany work.

A botanical scrapbook is a record of all the fascinating plants you see. There are many different ways to make one. Writing in extra details like where and when you saw each plant will make your scrapbook even more interesting.

Eco Explorer Kit List:

- **Empty notepad**
- **Pencils and crayons**
- **Heavy books**
- **Flower and tree identification books**
- **Paints and paintbrushes**
- **Paper tape**

BOTANICAL DRAWING

Record a plant without removing it from its home by using pencils or crayons to draw what you see in your scrapbook. Refer to your flower and tree books when adding labels.

FLOWER PRESSING

Place any flowers or leaves you collect inside a heavy book. Leave them there for a few weeks until they're completely flat, then stick them into your scrapbook. Jot down what they are and where you found them—and never pick more than a few flowers.

TREE BARK RUBBING

Hold a piece of paper against a tree trunk and rub a crayon all over it to make a print of the pattern. Bark patterns vary from one species to another, so try this with a few different types of tree to compare.

DANDELION BLOW PAINTING

Paint a page in your scrapbook any color you like, then blow a dandelion seedhead over the wet paint. The seeds will stick to create a beautiful piece of art that shows how seeds spread in the wind.

Recording your botanical finds like this can help you to learn all about the wonderful world of plants. You'll soon have a scrapbook bursting at the seams with information about all the different species you have found.

IN THE HOME

Like any other species, humans share habitats with other animals—and that includes inside our homes. It's not surprising that some creatures have adapted to living there when these warm, cozy ecosystems protect them from both predators and the weather.

DID YOU KNOW?
There are over 1.6 billion houses and flats in the world. That's a lot of potential habitats for wildlife!

DID YOU KNOW?
The average household throws away around 3,500 pieces of plastic every year.

DID YOU KNOW?

Studies have shown that there can be over 100 different species sharing our home at any one time.

No animal has adapted to living in our homes better than bugs. Spiders, ladybugs, woodlice, and lacewings are all common sightings in our homes.

Our homes not only provide habitat for other species, they're also one of the best places to start taking action to save the planet. Saving electricity, conserving water, and reducing single-use plastics can all be done there.

ADVENTURE CHALLENGE

Which bugs can you spot in your home? Peek in the corners of ceilings, under beds, behind furniture, and along carpet edges.

Look Out For:

Can you spot these animals in your home?

SPIDERS
A human home is the perfect habitat for many spiders. They are safe and warm, and there are plenty of smaller bugs to eat. Look for spider webs in ceiling corners.

MOTHS
If you leave a window open at night, you may find that moths will fly inside. They're attracted to your lights and mistake them for the moon, which they use to navigate.

REPTILES
In certain parts of the world, snakes and lizards can be a common house guest. They may crawl inside houses in search of prey or a warm nesting site.

BATS
Bats have been spotted roosting and sometimes even hibernating in the attics of houses. They are a protected animal in many countries, so you should take care not to disturb them.

Many animals have been able to adapt well to life inside our homes, but living there is quite different to living outside in the wild. Some animals may have to face threats in human homes that they've never dealt with before.

★ HUMAN-WILDLIFE CONFLICT

There's often conflict when humans and wildlife interact. Sadly, we often see creatures in our homes as dirty, dangerous, or scary. We should always take care around wildlife, but avoid killing or harming them as they're usually not as frightening as we might think.

★ ARTIFICIAL LIGHTING

The lights we use inside our homes can confuse animals, particularly ones who rely on moonlight, like moths. They can be tempted inside, only to become trapped there, struggling to find a way out again.

★ DOMESTIC PETS

Many bugs and small animals may enter our homes to escape from predators outside, but they're not always out of trouble. Pets like dogs and cats can harm them just as much as wild predators.

★ DISTURBANCE

Not all animals realize when they're entering human territory so it can be surprising when we disturb them. A female spider might spin her egg sac in a cozy house, only for us to vacuum it up.

HABITAT HERO: CELLAR SPIDERS

These gangly creatures, sometimes called Daddy Long Legs, may not be everyone's favorite house guest, but they can be useful because they hunt and eat much bigger house spiders.

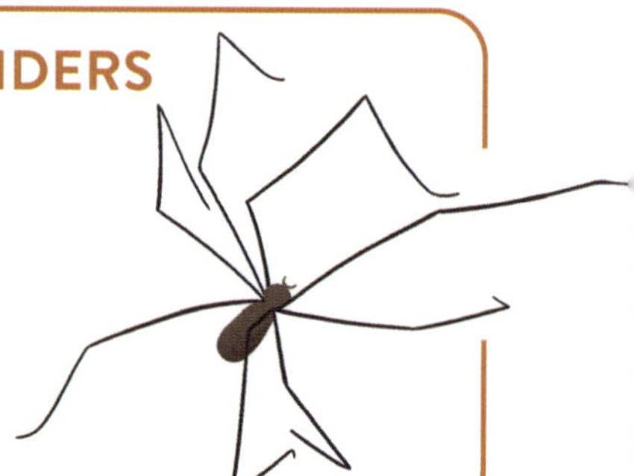

The best thing we can do as eco explorers is to remind people that the creatures who settle into our homes mean us no harm. Even animals that do pose a risk to us just need moving on safely and carefully.

RELEASE BUGS OUTSIDE

If you don't want to share your space with bugs, then release them safely outside rather than killing them. Place a glass over the top of them, then slide some paper underneath to keep them contained.

LET THEM BE

The best option is to just live with bugs and let them be. If they came inside for warmth or protection, taking them back outside puts them back at risk. Also, spiders eat lots of flies so they can be very handy!

DO YOUR CHORES

Lots of animals are attracted into our homes by the food waste and mess we leave there. To keep creatures like cockroaches and rodents out, make sure you keep your living spaces clean and tidy.

EDUCATE OTHERS

A lot of people fear bugs and pass this worry on. As an eco explorer, you can help to prevent this by telling everyone how amazing bugs are—and how some can actually benefit our homes.

ACTIVITY: GROW AN INDOOR HERB GARDEN

A great way to bring some nature inside your home, and to also live more sustainably, is to grow your own food. Most vegetables need outdoor space, but one food plant family in particular is perfect for growing indoors: herbs.

SUSTAINABLE LIVING
Store-bought vegetables have to be transported from farm to shop, which adds to air pollution. Growing your own food at home is much more sustainable than buying it from stores because it doesn't produce any pollution.

ROSEMARY has a woody, slightly peppery taste.

THYME has a minty, earthy taste.

OREGANO tastes slightly bitter and a little earthy.

MINT is sweet and leaves your tongue feeling cool.

SAGE has an earthy, slightly peppery taste.

CHIVES taste a bit like mild onions.

An indoor herb garden is a great alternative way to grow plants if you don't have a yard. You can even open a window and let pollinators come inside to visit your herbs. Garden centers have lots of wildlife-friendly herbs to choose from.

Eco Explorer Kit List:

- **Empty yogurt pots**
- **Potting soil**
- **Herb seeds**
- **Wooden popsticle sticks and a pen**
- **Water**
- **Compostable food wrap**

Step 1: Fill your pots with soil, leaving about 1 inch at the top. Then gently press the soil down.

Step 2: Sprinkle a few seeds into each pot, then cover them with a bit more soil. Only use one type of seed in each pot and poke in a popsticle stick with the name written on it.

Step 3: Lightly water your seeds and place your little herb garden on a sunny windowsill.

Step 4: To keep the seeds warm and moist and help them to sprout new shoots, cover each pot tightly with food wrap.

Step 5: The seeds should germinate after about 1–3 weeks. Once you see a small green shoot, you can remove the covering.

Now you have your very own indoor herb garden! Herbs are quite a quick growing plant, so they'll be big enough to harvest in no time. What will you cook with them first?

ACTIVITY: CONSTRUCT A WOODLOUSE HOUSE

Woodlice are an invertebrate that is quite commonly found in our homes. They're perfectly harmless though and won't hurt you or damage anything. These little creatures are detritivores and help to recycle the ecosystems they live in by eating plant material like dead leaves and rotting vegetables.

Unlike most other creatures, woodlice can safely eat harmful heavy metals found in soil such as lead and arsenic. By stopping these poisons from leaching into the groundwater and contaminating it, woodlice are real habitat heroes!

DID YOU KNOW?

With their 14 legs, woodlice are actually more closely related to crabs and lobsters than insects.

DID YOU KNOW?

Woodlice don't pee! Instead, they produce a strong-smelling gas called ammonia, which passes out through their exoskeleton.

DID YOU KNOW?

Some of the many nicknames given to woodlice around the world include roly polies, pill bugs, timberpigs, chiggy wigs, monkey peas, and cheesy bugs.

WHERE CAN YOU FIND YOUR WOODLICE?
Woodlice love dark, damp places, so look for them under things like paving slabs, plant pots, and any bits of dead wood and you'll be sure to find some.

Woodlice are fascinating creatures, and there may well be a lot more to learn about them than we already know. So why not build your own woodlouse house to study them up close?

Eco Explorer Kit List:

- **Small plastic container with a thin lid**
- **Scissors**
- **Pesticide-free soil**
- **Fallen leaves and dead wood**
- **Sticks and stones**
- **Raw vegetables such as lettuce, carrots, and potatoes**
- **Water spray bottle**

Step 1: Ask an adult to poke some holes in the container lid so the woodlice can breath. Then pour in a 1-inch layer of soil.

Step 2: Make perfect woodlouse substrate by shredding fallen leaves and smashing up dead wood, then mix these into the soil.

Step 3: Woodlice like dark places, so add lots of sticks, stones, fallen leaves, and dead wood to their enclosure to give them lots of places to hide.

Step 4: Woodlice will munch away on the dead leaves and wood, but you will need to supplement their diet by adding raw vegetables as well.

Step 5: Spray a mist of water over the whole enclosure every few days to keep it damp—just how woodlice like it!

All you need to do now is move some woodlice into your very own woodlouse house. They'll probably start breeding, so look out for their tiny babies in the substrate.

Don't forget to release your woodlice back out into the wild once you've finished watching them.

CONCLUSION

Whether you live next to the beach or in a city, near a woodland or in a small countryside village, there are plenty of things you can do to help your local ecosystems and become an expert eco explorer.

As eco explorers, it's our mission to ensure that the fragile balance of life on Earth is protected. By learning about the wonders of nature and how our lives impact it, we can help to reverse the consequences of deforestation, climate change, and habitat loss.

However, the best way we can have a positive impact on our environment is to actually keep our focus closer to home. Our yards, local green spaces, and even inside our homes are often the best places to start making a change.

The natural world is a magical place, full of all kinds of creatures, great and small—plants, animals, fungi, and bacteria all interact with one another and coexist in a delicate balance. Being an eco explorer is all about being part of that world and living in harmony with wildlife. It's about having fun in nature and enjoying the outdoors, while still respecting the ecosystems that support us.

So next time you find yourself outdoors, take a few moments to admire the flowers, listen to the buzz of the bees, or move a snail off the pavement and out of harm's way. That's what being an eco explorer is all about.

GLOSSARY

There are a lot of words in this book that may be tricky to understand. Here's a list of terms to learn that you can flick to anytime you're unsure of a word you read.

Agriculture: growing plants and farming animals for food.

Algae: tiny organisms that can build up in water and make it look green.

Altitude: how high a place is above sea level.

Amphibian: animals that spend their lives living both on land and in water.

Aphids: tiny insects that use their straw-like mouthparts to suck up plant sap.

Aquatic: animals that live in water.

Arid: environments that get little rain and are very dry.

Atmosphere: the layer of gas that surrounds Earth.

Biodegradable: materials that breakdown harmlessly and naturally in the environment over time.

Biodiversity: the variety of different organisms living in a particular habitat.

Botanist: a scientist who studies plants.

Brumation: a deep, sleep-like state that reptiles enter during the cold winter months.

Caching: hiding and storing food for later use.

Calorie: a way of measuring how much energy your body will receive from food or drink.

Carnivores: animals that eat other animals.

Climate change: changes to Earth's weather patterns that occur over time.

Compost: recycled organic matter that can be used to fertilize soil.

Convex lenses: glass that has an outwardly curving face and helps people to see things closer up.

Coniferous trees: trees that keep their leaves all year round.

Conserve protecting organisms and resources to make sure they are around in the future.

Consumer: people who buy and use products. Also refers to an organism that eats another organism.

Crustacean: a group of animals that includes crabs, lobsters, and woodlice.

Deciduous trees: trees that lose their leaves in the fall.

Decomposer: microorganisms that breakdown organic matter like dead plants and animals.

Deforestation: chopping down large areas of forest.

Dehydration: not having enough water in your body.

Detritivores: organisms that eat dead organisms and other waste materials like poop.

Dormant: a state of inactivity.

Driftwood: wood that has been washed ashore out of water.

Drought: a long period of very little rainfall.

Ecosystem: a community of lots of different organisms that live and interact with each other in a certain area.

Equator: an invisible line around the middle of Earth that divides it into two.

Erosion: soil and rock being worn away by either water or wind.

Estivation: a deep, sleep-like state that some animals enter during warm summer months.

Eutrophication: an increase of nutrients in water that leads to many problems for the organisms living there.

Evaporation: the process of turning a liquid to a gas through heat.

Exoskeleton: the hard outer covering that some animals have to protect their soft bodies inside.

Extinction: when a species completely dies out.

Exuvia: the shed exoskeleton of an insect left behind as it moults and grows.

Fertilizer: chemicals that can be added to soil to help plants grow better.

Food chain: the sequence in which organisms eat other organisms in an ecosystem, showing the order that they depend on each other for food.

Germinate: when a seed first sprouts a tiny shoot.

Global warming: an increase in Earth's average temperature.

Greenhouse gases: gases that trap heat in the Earth's atmosphere and warm it up like a greenhouse.

Graywater: used water from sinks, baths and showers.

Habitat: the area where an organism lives.

Herbivores: animals that eat plants.

Hermaphrodites: animals that have both male and female reproductive organs.

Hibernaculum: a safe place for animals to hibernate in.

Hibernation: a deep, sleep-like state that some animals enter during cold winter months.

Insectivores: animals that eat insects.

Invasive species: organisms that come from elsewhere and can harm the local wildlife.

Invertebrates: animals that don't have a backbone, such as insects and spiders.

Latitude: how far away a place is from the equator.

Light pollution: too much man-made light in the night sky that can cause harm to wildlife.

Light years: the distance that light can travel in a year.

Mammal: a type of animal that has fur or hair, provides milk for its babies and usually gives birth to live young. Dogs, elephants, whales, and humans are mammals.

Marine: related to or found in the sea.

Microscopic: something so small that you need a microscope to see it.

Migrate: moving to a different part of the world during different seasons.

Monoculture: growing only one type of crop in an area.

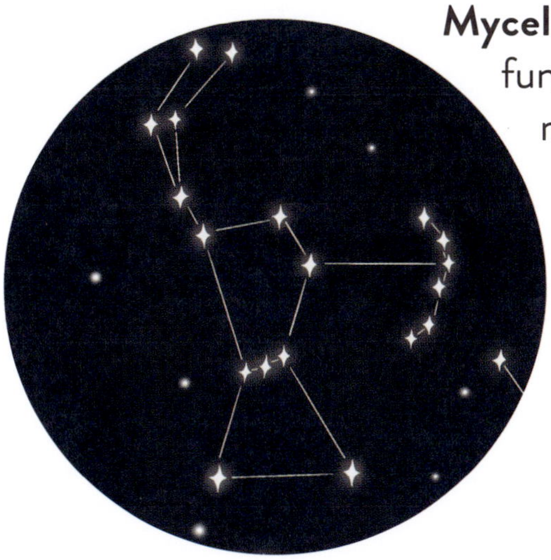

Mycelium: the thread-like, underground part of a fungus that absorbs nutrients and sends messages.

NASA: National Aeronautics and Space Administration, an organization in the USA that studies and explores space.

Nocturnal: animals that sleep during the day and are active at night.

Organism: the name we give to any form of life. It could be a plant, an animal, a fungus or even bacteria.

Permafrost: soil that is permanently frozen.

Pest: an organism that is annoying or damaging to the ecosystem.

Pesticide: a chemical that is used to kill certain creatures that harm crops.

pH: how acidic or alkaline something is.

Photosynthesis: the process by which plants use sunlight to make their own food.

Plankton: tiny organisms that float around in the water and are food for many bigger animals.

Pollinators: animals that help plants to reproduce by moving pollen from one flower to another.

Pollution: substances released that cause harm to the environment and the organisms living there.

Predators: animals that hunt and eat other animals.

Proteins: a type of nutrient that is needed in your body for growth and repair.

Renewable resource: something we take from the environment that can be replaced naturally and won't run out, such as sunlight and wind.

Rural: another word for countryside, where there are small settlements and lots of agriculture taking place.

Settlements: places where humans live, such as cities, towns, and villages.

Spores: tiny particles that fungi use in order to reproduce.

Substrate: the ground surface upon which an organism lives or grows.

Sustainability: using resources in a way that keeps them around for the future and doesn't harm the planet.

Synthetic fabric: man-made fabrics created using chemicals.

Temperate: when the weather is not extremely hot or cold.

Thaw: the process of ice melting.

Tree canopy: the layer of branches and leaves at the very top of a tree.

Torpor: a state of mental and physical inactivity.

Urbanization: the process of cities expanding as more and more people move into them.

Vegetation: the plants that grow in a particular ecosystem.

Xerophiles: organisms that can survive in dry environments.

MOON
BIRD

We publish empowering and enchanting books to open children's eyes to the wonder of the world and help them grow and thrive. Our beautiful, groundbreaking books encourage curiosity, resilience and inclusivity, and help kids manage their own feelings and find their own special path in life.